A DAILY DOSE OF

BLESSINGS

*A daily journal for
appreciating life's gifts*

PETER PAUPER PRESS, INC.
WHITE PLAINS, NEW YORK

PETER PAUPER PRESS
Fine Books and Gifts Since 1928

Our Company

In 1928, at the age of twenty-two, Peter Beilenson began printing books on a small press in the basement of his parents' home in Larchmont, New York. Peter—and later, his wife, Edna—sought to create fine books that sold at "prices even a pauper could afford."

Today, still family owned and operated, Peter Pauper Press continues to honor our founders' legacy—and our customers' expectations—of beauty, quality, and value.

Designed by Heather Zschock
Cover illustration © Jill McDonald | Jennifer Nelson Artists, Inc.

Copyright © 2019
Peter Pauper Press, Inc.
202 Mamaroneck Avenue
White Plains, NY 10601 USA
All rights reserved
ISBN 978-1-4413-2946-2
Printed in China
7 6 5 4 3 2 1

Visit us at www.peterpauper.com

This is the day the LORD has made.
We will rejoice and be glad in it.

Psalm 118:24 (NKJV)

*L*ife is made of small blessings, but these blessings don't always come in the ways we'd expect.

Keeping a daily journal in which you note the blessings of the day helps cultivate an awareness and a sense of gratitude. It trains you to pay attention to the many gifts life serves up, whether it be a bird song at dawn or an answered prayer.

A blessing can be an unexpected stroke of luck, or it can be a good outcome at the end of a struggle. It can be a blessing received or a blessing given. When we share kindness, hope, and goodness with others, we light a candle against the darkness. To bless those around us takes conscious living, which is where this journal comes in.

Each day, notice the small golden moments in your life, and strive to give back when you can. Reach for this journal in the evenings to write down all the ways you were blessed that day and all the ways you blessed others. Make it a habit to spread the joy as you appreciate the blessings that show up in your life every day.

Happy journaling, and may blessings abound!

MY BLESSINGS LIST

How I consider myself to be blessed as I start my journey:

Ways I can bestow blessings on others this year:

Today's blessings: _____ Date: _____

_____

_____

_____

_____

_____

_____

Today's blessings: _____ Date: _____

_____

_____

_____

_____

_____

_____

Today's blessings: _____ Date: _____

_____

_____

_____

_____

_____

_____

Today's blessings: _____ Date: _____

_____

_____

_____

_____

_____

_____

Today's blessings: _____ Date: _____

_____

_____

_____

_____

_____

_____

How I blessed others this week: _____

_____

_____

_____

_____

_____

_____

_____

Today's blessings: _____ Date: _____

_____

_____

_____

_____

_____

Today's blessings: _____ Date: _____

_____

_____

_____

_____

_____

Today's blessings: _____ Date: _____

_____

_____

_____

_____

_____

Today's blessings: _____ Date: _____

_____

_____

_____

_____

_____

_____

Today's blessings: _____ Date: _____

_____

_____

_____

_____

_____

How I blessed others this week: _____

_____

_____

_____

_____

_____

_____

Today's blessings: _____ Date: _____

_____

_____

_____

_____

_____

_____

Today's blessings: _____ Date: _____

_____

_____

_____

_____

_____

_____

Today's blessings: _____ Date: _____

_____

_____

_____

_____

_____

_____

Today's blessings: _____   Date: _____

_____

_____

_____

_____

_____

_____

Today's blessings: _____   Date: _____

_____

_____

_____

_____

_____

How I blessed others this week: _____

_____

_____

_____

_____

_____

_____

Today's blessings: _____   Date: _____

_____

_____

_____

_____

_____

_____

Today's blessings: _____   Date: _____

_____

_____

_____

_____

_____

_____

Today's blessings: _____   Date: _____

_____

_____

_____

_____

_____

_____

Today's blessings: _____ Date: _____

_____

_____

_____

_____

_____

Today's blessings: _____ Date: _____

_____

_____

_____

_____

_____

How I blessed others this week: _____

_____

_____

_____

_____

_____

Today's blessings: _____ Date: _____

_____

_____

_____

_____

_____

_____

Today's blessings: _____ Date: _____

_____

_____

_____

_____

_____

_____

Today's blessings: _____ Date: _____

_____

_____

_____

_____

_____

_____

Today's blessings: _____ Date: _____

_____

_____

_____

_____

_____

_____

Today's blessings: _____ Date: _____

_____

_____

_____

_____

_____

_____

How I blessed others this week: _____

_____

_____

_____

_____

_____

_____

Today's blessings: _____ Date: _____

_____

_____

_____

_____

_____

Today's blessings: _____ Date: _____

_____

_____

_____

_____

_____

Today's blessings: _____ Date: _____

_____

_____

_____

_____

_____

Today's blessings: _____ Date: _____

_____

_____

_____

_____

_____

_____

Today's blessings: _____ Date: _____

_____

_____

_____

_____

_____

How I blessed others this week:

_____

_____

_____

_____

_____

_____

So let's not get tired of
doing what is good.
At just the right time we will
reap a harvest of blessing
if we don't give up.

Galatians 6:9 (NLT)

People I am blessed with:

Today's blessings: _____ Date: _____

_____

_____

_____

_____

_____

Today's blessings: _____ Date: _____

_____

_____

_____

_____

_____

Today's blessings: _____ Date: _____

_____

_____

_____

_____

_____

Today's blessings: _____ Date: _____

_____

_____

_____

_____

_____

_____

Today's blessings: _____ Date: _____

_____

_____

_____

_____

_____

How I blessed others this week: _____

_____

_____

_____

_____

_____

_____

Today's blessings: _____ Date: _____

_____

_____

_____

_____

_____

_____

Today's blessings: _____ Date: _____

_____

_____

_____

_____

_____

_____

Today's blessings: _____ Date: _____

_____

_____

_____

_____

_____

_____

Today's blessings: _____   Date: _____

_____

_____

_____

_____

_____

_____

Today's blessings: _____   Date: _____

_____

_____

_____

_____

_____

How I blessed others this week: _____

Today's blessings: _____ Date: _____

_____

_____

_____

_____

_____

_____

Today's blessings: _____ Date: _____

_____

_____

_____

_____

_____

Today's blessings: _____ Date: _____

_____

_____

_____

_____

_____

_____

Today's blessings: _____ Date: _____

_____

_____

_____

_____

_____

Today's blessings: _____ Date: _____

_____

_____

_____

_____

_____

How I blessed others this week: _____

_____

_____

_____

_____

_____

Today's blessings: _____ Date: _____

_____

_____

_____

_____

_____

_____

Today's blessings: _____ Date: _____

_____

_____

_____

_____

_____

_____

Today's blessings: _____ Date: _____

_____

_____

_____

_____

_____

_____

Today's blessings: _____ Date: _____

_____

_____

_____

_____

_____

_____

Today's blessings: _____ Date: _____

_____

_____

_____

_____

_____

How I blessed others this week: _____

_____

_____

_____

_____

_____

_____

Today's blessings: _____ Date: _____

_____

_____

_____

_____

_____

_____

Today's blessings: _____ Date: _____

_____

_____

_____

_____

_____

_____

Today's blessings: _____ Date: _____

_____

_____

_____

_____

_____

_____

Today's blessings: _____ Date: _____

_____

_____

_____

_____

_____

_____

Today's blessings: _____ Date: _____

_____

_____

_____

_____

_____

_____

How I blessed others this week: _____

_____

_____

_____

_____

_____

_____

Today's blessings: _____ Date: _____

_____

_____

_____

_____

_____

_____

Today's blessings: _____ Date: _____

_____

_____

_____

_____

_____

_____

Today's blessings: _____ Date: _____

_____

_____

_____

_____

_____

_____

Today's blessings: _____ Date: _____

_____
_____
_____
_____
_____
_____

Today's blessings: _____ Date: _____

_____
_____
_____
_____
_____

How I blessed others this week: _____

_____
_____
_____
_____
_____
_____

I thank you God for
most this amazing day:
for the leaping greenly
spirits of trees and
a blue true dream of sky;
and for everything which is
natural, which is infinite,
which is yes.

E. E. Cummings

Things I am blessed with:

Today's blessings: _____ Date: _____

Today's blessings: _____ Date: _____

Today's blessings: _____ Date: _____

Today's blessings: _____ Date: _____

_____

_____

_____

_____

_____

_____

Today's blessings: _____ Date: _____

_____

_____

_____

_____

_____

_____

How I blessed others this week: _____

_____

_____

_____

_____

_____

_____

Today's blessings: _____ Date: _____

_____

_____

_____

_____

_____

_____

Today's blessings: _____ Date: _____

_____

_____

_____

_____

_____

_____

Today's blessings: _____ Date: _____

_____

_____

_____

_____

_____

_____

Today's blessings: _____ Date: _____

_____

_____

_____

_____

_____

Today's blessings: _____ Date: _____

_____

_____

_____

_____

_____

How I blessed others this week:

_____

_____

_____

_____

_____

_____

Today's blessings: _____ Date: _____

Today's blessings: _____ Date: _____

Today's blessings: _____ Date: _____

Today's blessings: _____ Date: _____

_____

_____

_____

_____

_____

_____

Today's blessings: _____ Date: _____

_____

_____

_____

_____

_____

_____

How I blessed others this week: _____

_____

_____

_____

_____

_____

_____

Today's blessings: _____ Date: _____

Today's blessings: _____ Date: _____

Today's blessings: _____ Date: _____

Today's blessings: _____ Date: _____

_____

_____

_____

_____

_____

_____

Today's blessings: _____ Date: _____

_____

_____

_____

_____

_____

_____

How I blessed others this week: _____

Today's blessings: _____ Date: _____

_____

_____

_____

_____

_____

_____

Today's blessings: _____ Date: _____

_____

_____

_____

_____

_____

_____

Today's blessings: _____ Date: _____

_____

_____

_____

_____

_____

_____

Today's blessings: _____ Date: _____

_____

_____

_____

_____

_____

_____

Today's blessings: _____ Date: _____

_____

_____

_____

_____

_____

_____

How I blessed others this week: _____

_____

_____

_____

_____

_____

_____

Today's blessings: _____ Date: _____

_____
_____
_____
_____
_____
_____

Today's blessings: _____ Date: _____

_____
_____
_____
_____
_____
_____

Today's blessings: _____ Date: _____

_____
_____
_____
_____
_____
_____

Today's blessings: _____ Date: _____

_____
_____
_____
_____
_____
_____

Today's blessings: _____ Date: _____

_____
_____
_____
_____
_____

How I blessed others this week: _____

_____
_____
_____
_____
_____
_____

*In all thy ways
acknowledge him,
and he shall
direct thy paths.*

Proverbs 3:6 (KJV)

Counting my blessings:

Today's blessings: _____ Date: _____

_____

_____

_____

_____

_____

_____

Today's blessings: _____ Date: _____

_____

_____

_____

_____

_____

_____

Today's blessings: _____ Date: _____

_____

_____

_____

_____

_____

_____

Today's blessings: _____ Date: _____

_____

_____

_____

_____

_____

Today's blessings: _____ Date: _____

_____

_____

_____

_____

_____

How I blessed others this week: _____

Today's blessings: _____ Date: _____

_____

_____

_____

_____

_____

_____

Today's blessings: _____ Date: _____

_____

_____

_____

_____

_____

_____

Today's blessings: _____ Date: _____

_____

_____

_____

_____

_____

_____

Today's blessings: _____ Date: _____

_____

_____

_____

_____

_____

_____

Today's blessings: _____ Date: _____

_____

_____

_____

_____

_____

How I blessed others this week: _____

_____

_____

_____

_____

_____

_____

Today's blessings: _____ Date: _____

Today's blessings: _____ Date: _____

Today's blessings: _____ Date: _____

Today's blessings: _____ Date: _____

_____

_____

_____

_____

_____

_____

Today's blessings: _____ Date: _____

_____

_____

_____

_____

_____

How I blessed others this week: _____

_____

_____

_____

_____

_____

Today's blessings: _____ Date: _____

_____

_____

_____

_____

_____

_____

Today's blessings: _____ Date: _____

_____

_____

_____

_____

_____

_____

Today's blessings: _____ Date: _____

_____

_____

_____

_____

_____

_____

Today's blessings: _____ Date: _____

_____

_____

_____

_____

_____

_____

Today's blessings: _____ Date: _____

_____

_____

_____

_____

_____

How I blessed others this week:

Today's blessings: _____ Date: _____

_____

_____

_____

_____

_____

_____

Today's blessings: _____ Date: _____

_____

_____

_____

_____

_____

Today's blessings: _____ Date: _____

_____

_____

_____

_____

_____

_____

Today's blessings: _____ Date: _____

_____

_____

_____

_____

_____

Today's blessings: _____ Date: _____

_____

_____

_____

_____

_____

How I blessed others this week:

_____

_____

_____

_____

_____

_____

Today's blessings: _____ Date: _____

_____

_____

_____

_____

_____

_____

Today's blessings: _____ Date: _____

_____

_____

_____

_____

_____

_____

Today's blessings: _____ Date: _____

_____

_____

_____

_____

_____

_____

Today's blessings: _____ Date: _____

_____

_____

_____

_____

_____

_____

Today's blessings: _____ Date: _____

_____

_____

_____

_____

_____

How I blessed others this week: _____

_____

_____

_____

_____

_____

When we give cheerfully
and accept gratefully,
everyone is blessed.

Maya Angelou

Offering up special blessings for family and friends:

Today's blessings: _____ Date: _____

_____

_____

_____

_____

_____

_____

Today's blessings: _____ Date: _____

_____

_____

_____

_____

_____

_____

Today's blessings: _____ Date: _____

_____

_____

_____

_____

_____

_____

Today's blessings: _____ Date: _____

_____

_____

_____

_____

_____

_____

_____

Today's blessings: _____ Date: _____

_____

_____

_____

_____

_____

How I blessed others this week: _____

_____

_____

_____

_____

_____

Today's blessings: _____ Date: _____

_____

_____

_____

_____

_____

_____

Today's blessings: _____ Date: _____

_____

_____

_____

_____

_____

_____

Today's blessings: _____ Date: _____

_____

_____

_____

_____

_____

_____

Today's blessings: _____ Date: _____

_____
_____
_____
_____
_____
_____

Today's blessings: _____ Date: _____

_____
_____
_____
_____
_____

How I blessed others this week: _____

_____
_____
_____
_____
_____
_____

Today's blessings: _____   Date: _____

_____

_____

_____

_____

_____

_____

Today's blessings: _____   Date: _____

_____

_____

_____

_____

_____

_____

Today's blessings: _____   Date: _____

_____

_____

_____

_____

_____

_____

Today's blessings: _____ Date: _____

_____

_____

_____

_____

_____

_____

Today's blessings: _____ Date: _____

_____

_____

_____

_____

_____

How I blessed others this week: _____

_____

_____

_____

_____

_____

_____

Today's blessings: _____ Date: _____

Today's blessings: _____ Date: _____

Today's blessings: _____ Date: _____

Today's blessings: _____ Date: _____

_____

_____

_____

_____

_____

Today's blessings: _____ Date: _____

_____

_____

_____

_____

_____

How I blessed others this week: _____

Today's blessings: _____   Date: _____

_____

_____

_____

_____

_____

_____

Today's blessings: _____   Date: _____

_____

_____

_____

_____

_____

_____

Today's blessings: _____   Date: _____

_____

_____

_____

_____

_____

_____

Today's blessings: _____ Date: _____

_____

_____

_____

_____

_____

_____

Today's blessings: _____ Date: _____

_____

_____

_____

_____

_____

How I blessed others this week: _____

_____

_____

_____

_____

_____

_____

Today's blessings: _____ Date: _____

_____

_____

_____

_____

_____

_____

Today's blessings: _____ Date: _____

_____

_____

_____

_____

_____

_____

Today's blessings: _____ Date: _____

_____

_____

_____

_____

_____

_____

Today's blessings: _____ Date: _____

_____

_____

_____

_____

_____

Today's blessings: _____ Date: _____

_____

_____

_____

_____

_____

How I blessed others this week: _____

_____

_____

_____

_____

When we lose one
blessing, another is
often most unexpectedly
given in its place.

C. S. Lewis

How unexpected changes have led to blessings:

Today's blessings: _____ Date: _____

_____
_____
_____
_____
_____
_____
_____

Today's blessings: _____ Date: _____

_____
_____
_____
_____
_____
_____
_____

Today's blessings: _____ Date: _____

_____
_____
_____
_____
_____
_____
_____

Today's blessings: _____ Date: _____

_____

_____

_____

_____

_____

_____

Today's blessings: _____ Date: _____

_____

_____

_____

_____

_____

_____

How I blessed others this week: _____

_____

_____

_____

_____

_____

_____

Today's blessings: _____ Date: _____

_____

_____

_____

_____

_____

_____

Today's blessings: _____ Date: _____

_____

_____

_____

_____

_____

_____

Today's blessings: _____ Date: _____

_____

_____

_____

_____

_____

_____

Today's blessings: _____ Date: _____

_____

_____

_____

_____

_____

Today's blessings: _____ Date: _____

_____

_____

_____

_____

How I blessed others this week: _____

_____

_____

_____

_____

Today's blessings: _____ Date: _____

_____

_____

_____

_____

_____

Today's blessings: _____ Date: _____

_____

_____

_____

_____

_____

Today's blessings: _____ Date: _____

_____

_____

_____

_____

_____

Today's blessings: _____ Date: _____

_____

_____

_____

_____

_____

_____

Today's blessings: _____ Date: _____

_____

_____

_____

_____

_____

How I blessed others this week: _____

_____

_____

_____

_____

_____

Today's blessings: _____ Date: _____

_____
_____
_____
_____
_____
_____

Today's blessings: _____ Date: _____

_____
_____
_____
_____
_____
_____

Today's blessings: _____ Date: _____

_____
_____
_____
_____
_____
_____

Today's blessings: _____ Date: _____

_____

_____

_____

_____

_____

_____

Today's blessings: _____ Date: _____

_____

_____

_____

_____

_____

How I blessed others this week:

_____

_____

_____

_____

_____

Today's blessings: _____ Date: _____

_____

_____

_____

_____

_____

_____

Today's blessings: _____ Date: _____

_____

_____

_____

_____

_____

_____

Today's blessings: _____ Date: _____

_____

_____

_____

_____

_____

_____

Today's blessings: _____ Date: _____

_____

_____

_____

_____

_____

_____

Today's blessings: _____ Date: _____

_____

_____

_____

_____

_____

_____

How I blessed others this week: _____

_____

_____

_____

_____

_____

_____

Today's blessings: _____ Date: _____

Today's blessings: _____ Date: _____

Today's blessings: _____ Date: _____

Today's blessings: _____ Date: _____

_____

_____

_____

_____

_____

_____

Today's blessings: _____ Date: _____

_____

_____

_____

_____

_____

_____

How I blessed others this week: _____

_____

_____

_____

_____

_____

Kind words are a
creative force, a power
that concurs in the
building up of all that
is good, and energy
that showers blessings
upon the world.

Lawrence G. Lovasik

Ways I can show kindness this week:

Today's blessings: _____ Date: _____

_____

_____

_____

_____

_____

_____

Today's blessings: _____ Date: _____

_____

_____

_____

_____

_____

_____

Today's blessings: _____ Date: _____

_____

_____

_____

_____

_____

_____

Today's blessings: _____ Date: _____

_____

_____

_____

_____

_____

_____

Today's blessings: _____ Date: _____

_____

_____

_____

_____

_____

How I blessed others this week: _____

_____

_____

_____

_____

_____

Today's blessings: _____ Date: _____

Today's blessings: _____ Date: _____

Today's blessings: _____ Date: _____

Today's blessings: _____ Date: _____

_____

_____

_____

_____

_____

_____

Today's blessings: _____ Date: _____

_____

_____

_____

_____

_____

How I blessed others this week: _____

_____

_____

_____

_____

_____

Today's blessings: _____ Date: _____

_____

_____

_____

_____

_____

_____

Today's blessings: _____ Date: _____

_____

_____

_____

_____

_____

_____

Today's blessings: _____ Date: _____

_____

_____

_____

_____

_____

_____

Today's blessings: _____ Date: _____

_____

_____

_____

_____

_____

_____

Today's blessings: _____ Date: _____

_____

_____

_____

_____

_____

How I blessed others this week:
_____

_____

_____

_____

_____

_____

Today's blessings: _____ Date: _____

_____

_____

_____

_____

_____

_____

Today's blessings: _____ Date: _____

_____

_____

_____

_____

_____

_____

Today's blessings: _____ Date: _____

_____

_____

_____

_____

_____

_____

Today's blessings: _____ Date: _____

_____

_____

_____

_____

_____

_____

Today's blessings: _____ Date: _____

_____

_____

_____

_____

_____

How I blessed others this week: _____

_____

_____

_____

_____

_____

_____

Today's blessings: _____ Date: _____

_____

_____

_____

_____

_____

Today's blessings: _____ Date: _____

_____

_____

_____

_____

_____

Today's blessings: _____ Date: _____

_____

_____

_____

_____

_____

Today's blessings: _____ Date: _____

_____

_____

_____

_____

_____

_____

Today's blessings: _____ Date: _____

_____

_____

_____

_____

_____

_____

How I blessed others this week: _____

_____

_____

_____

_____

_____

_____

Today's blessings: _____ Date: _____

Today's blessings: _____ Date: _____

Today's blessings: _____ Date: _____

Today's blessings: _____ Date: _____

_____

_____

_____

_____

_____

_____

Today's blessings: _____ Date: _____

_____

_____

_____

_____

How I blessed others this week: _____

_____

_____

_____

_____

_____

For God has not given
us a spirit of fear,
but of power and of
love and of a
sound mind.

2 Timothy 1:7 (NKJV)

I use the blessings of power, love, and sound mind to:

Today's blessings: _____ Date: _____

_____

_____

_____

_____

_____

_____

Today's blessings: _____ Date: _____

_____

_____

_____

_____

_____

_____

Today's blessings: _____ Date: _____

_____

_____

_____

_____

_____

_____

Today's blessings: _____ Date: _____

_____

_____

_____

_____

_____

Today's blessings: _____ Date: _____

_____

_____

_____

_____

How I blessed others this week: _____

_____

_____

_____

_____

_____

Today's blessings: _____ Date: _____

Today's blessings: _____ Date: _____

Today's blessings: _____ Date: _____

Today's blessings: _____ Date: _____

_____

_____

_____

_____

_____

Today's blessings: _____ Date: _____

_____

_____

_____

_____

_____

How I blessed others this week:

Today's blessings: _____ Date: _____

_____

_____

_____

_____

_____

_____

Today's blessings: _____ Date: _____

_____

_____

_____

_____

_____

_____

Today's blessings: _____ Date: _____

_____

_____

_____

_____

_____

_____

Today's blessings: _____ Date: _____

_____

_____

_____

_____

_____

Today's blessings: _____ Date: _____

_____

_____

_____

_____

_____

How I blessed others this week: _____

_____

_____

_____

_____

_____

_____

Today's blessings: _____ Date: _____

_____

_____

_____

_____

_____

Today's blessings: _____ Date: _____

_____

_____

_____

_____

_____

Today's blessings: _____ Date: _____

_____

_____

_____

_____

_____

_____

Today's blessings: _____ Date: _____

_____

_____

_____

_____

_____

_____

Today's blessings: _____ Date: _____

_____

_____

_____

_____

_____

How I blessed others this week:

Today's blessings: _____ Date: _____

_____

_____

_____

_____

_____

Today's blessings: _____ Date: _____

_____

_____

_____

_____

_____

Today's blessings: _____ Date: _____

_____

_____

_____

_____

_____

Today's blessings: _____   Date: _____

_____

_____

_____

_____

_____

Today's blessings: _____   Date: _____

_____

_____

_____

_____

_____

How I blessed others this week:

Today's blessings: _____ Date: _____

_____

_____

_____

_____

_____

_____

Today's blessings: _____ Date: _____

_____

_____

_____

_____

_____

_____

Today's blessings: _____ Date: _____

_____

_____

_____

_____

_____

_____

Today's blessings: _____ Date: _____

Today's blessings: _____ Date: _____

How I blessed others this week: _____

*When you are grateful—
when you can see
what you have—
you unlock blessings
to flow in your life.*

Suze Orman

I am grateful for:

Today's blessings: _____ Date: _____

_____

_____

_____

_____

_____

_____

Today's blessings: _____ Date: _____

_____

_____

_____

_____

_____

_____

Today's blessings: _____ Date: _____

_____

_____

_____

_____

_____

_____

Today's blessings: _____ Date: _____

_____

_____

_____

_____

_____

_____

Today's blessings: _____ Date: _____

_____

_____

_____

_____

_____

_____

How I blessed others this week: _____

_____

_____

_____

_____

_____

Today's blessings: _____ Date: _____

_____

_____

_____

_____

_____

_____

Today's blessings: _____ Date: _____

_____

_____

_____

_____

_____

Today's blessings: _____ Date: _____

_____

_____

_____

_____

_____

_____

Today's blessings: _____ Date: _____

_____

_____

_____

_____

_____

Today's blessings: _____ Date: _____

_____

_____

_____

_____

_____

How I blessed others this week: _____

_____

_____

_____

_____

_____

_____

Today's blessings: _____ Date: _____

_____

_____

_____

_____

_____

Today's blessings: _____ Date: _____

_____

_____

_____

_____

_____

Today's blessings: _____ Date: _____

_____

_____

_____

_____

_____

Today's blessings: _____ Date: _____

_____

_____

_____

_____

_____

_____

Today's blessings: _____ Date: _____

_____

_____

_____

_____

_____

_____

How I blessed others this week: _____

_____

_____

_____

_____

_____

_____

Today's blessings: _____   Date: _____

_____

_____

_____

_____

_____

Today's blessings: _____   Date: _____

_____

_____

_____

_____

_____

Today's blessings: _____   Date: _____

_____

_____

_____

_____

_____

Today's blessings: _____ Date: _____

_____

_____

_____

_____

_____

Today's blessings: _____ Date: _____

_____

_____

_____

_____

_____

How I blessed others this week: _____

_____

_____

_____

_____

_____

Today's blessings: _____ Date: _____

_____

_____

_____

_____

_____

_____

Today's blessings: _____ Date: _____

_____

_____

_____

_____

_____

_____

Today's blessings: _____ Date: _____

_____

_____

_____

_____

_____

_____

Today's blessings: _____ Date: _____

Today's blessings: _____ Date: _____

How I blessed others this week: _____

Today's blessings: _____ Date: _____

Today's blessings: _____ Date: _____

Today's blessings: _____ Date: _____

Today's blessings: _____ Date: _____

_____

_____

_____

_____

_____

_____

Today's blessings: _____ Date: _____

_____

_____

_____

_____

_____

How I blessed others this week: _____

The Lord bless you
and keep you;
the Lord make his face
shine on you and be
gracious to you;
the Lord turn his face
toward you and give
you peace.

Numbers 6:24-26 (NIV)

How grace shows up in my life:

Today's blessings: _____ Date: _____

Today's blessings: _____ Date: _____

Today's blessings: _____ Date: _____

Today's blessings: _____ Date: _____

_____
_____
_____
_____
_____
_____

Today's blessings: _____ Date: _____

_____
_____
_____
_____
_____
_____

How I blessed others this week: _____
_____
_____
_____
_____
_____
_____

Today's blessings: _____ Date: _____

_____

_____

_____

_____

_____

Today's blessings: _____ Date: _____

_____

_____

_____

_____

_____

Today's blessings: _____ Date: _____

_____

_____

_____

_____

_____

Today's blessings: _____ Date: _____

Today's blessings: _____ Date: _____

How I blessed others this week:

Today's blessings: _____ Date: _____

_____

_____

_____

_____

_____

_____

_____

Today's blessings: _____ Date: _____

_____

_____

_____

_____

_____

_____

_____

Today's blessings: _____ Date: _____

_____

_____

_____

_____

_____

_____

Today's blessings: _____ Date: _____

_____

_____

_____

_____

_____

_____

Today's blessings: _____ Date: _____

_____

_____

_____

_____

_____

_____

How I blessed others this week: _____

_____

_____

_____

_____

_____

_____

_____

Today's blessings: _____ Date: _____

_____

_____

_____

_____

_____

_____

Today's blessings: _____ Date: _____

_____

_____

_____

_____

_____

_____

Today's blessings: _____ Date: _____

_____

_____

_____

_____

_____

_____

Today's blessings: _____ Date: _____

_____

_____

_____

_____

_____

Today's blessings: _____ Date: _____

_____

_____

_____

_____

_____

How I blessed others this week: _____

_____

_____

_____

_____

_____

_____

Today's blessings: _____ Date: _____

Today's blessings: _____ Date: _____

Today's blessings: _____ Date: _____

Today's blessings: _____ Date: _____

_____
_____
_____
_____
_____
_____

Today's blessings: _____ Date: _____

_____
_____
_____
_____
_____
_____

How I blessed others this week: _____

_____
_____
_____
_____
_____
_____

Today's blessings: _____ Date: _____

_____

_____

_____

_____

_____

_____

Today's blessings: _____ Date: _____

_____

_____

_____

_____

_____

_____

Today's blessings: _____ Date: _____

_____

_____

_____

_____

_____

_____

Today's blessings: _____ Date: _____

_____

_____

_____

_____

_____

_____

Today's blessings: _____ Date: _____

_____

_____

_____

_____

_____

_____

How I blessed others this week: _____

_____

_____

_____

_____

_____

_____

Finally, brethren,
whatever is true, whatever is
honorable, whatever is just,
whatever is pure, whatever is
lovely, whatever is gracious,
if there is any excellence,
if there is anything worthy
of praise, think about
these things.

Philippians 4:8 (RSV)

Scriptural Sources: